DOMINOES

William Tell and Other Stories

STARTER LEVEL   250 HEADWORDS

OXFORD
UNIVERSITY PRESS

Great Clarendon Street, Oxford OX2 6DP

Oxford University Press is a department of the University of Oxford.
It furthers the University's objective of excellence in research, scholarship,
and education by publishing worldwide in

Oxford New York

Auckland Cape Town Dar es Salaam Hong Kong Karachi
Kuala Lumpur Madrid Melbourne Mexico City Nairobi
New Delhi Shanghai Taipei Toronto

With offices in

Argentina Austria Brazil Chile Czech Republic France Greece
Guatemala Hungary Italy Japan Poland Portugal Singapore
South Korea Switzerland Thailand Turkey Ukraine Vietnam

OXFORD and OXFORD ENGLISH are registered trade marks of
Oxford University Press in the UK and in certain other countries

This edition © Oxford University Press 2010

The moral rights of the author have been asserted

Database right Oxford University Press (maker)

First published in Dominoes 2002

2014 2013 2012 2011 2010

10 9 8 7 6 5 4 3 2 1

ISBN: 978 0 19 424703 0 BOOK
ISBN: 978 0 19 424667 5 BOOK AND MULTIROM PACK
MULTIROM NOT AVAILABLE SEPARATELY

No unauthorized photocopying

Printed in China

ACKNOWLEDGEMENTS

Illustrations by: Adam Stower

The publisher would like to thank the following for permission to reproduce photographs: Britain on
View pp iv & 7 (Tower Bridge London), 7 (Yeoman Warder), 7 (Radcliffe Camera Oxford),
40 (Maypole dancing); Corbis pp iv (Dragon lantern/Bohemian Nomad Picturemakers), iv
(Folk dancers/Barry Lewis), 7 (Charles II/Bettmann), 25 (Abraham Lincoln/Bettmann), 41
(Daffodils/Bill Ross); Getty Images pp iv (Shawnee tribesman/Owen Franken), iv (Cattle
grazing/Stephen Studd/Stone), 25 (Oil rig/Frank Whitney/Image Bank), 25 (Red apples/Nick
Gunderson), 40 (Hot cross buns/Paul Webster); Reuters Pictures p 41 (Saint Patrick's Day
parade/Brad Rickerby); Ronald Grant Archive p 39 (*Robin Hood Prince of Thieves*/Warner Bros);
Scottish Viewpoint p 41 (Man wearing kilt).

Cover: Getty Images (boy with arrow through apple/Henrik Sorensen)

DOMINOES

Series Editors: Bill Bowler and Sue Parminter

William Tell and Other Stories

Retold by John Escott

Illustrated by Adam Stower

John Escott has written many books for readers of all ages, and particularly enjoys writing crime and mystery thrillers. He was born in the west of England, but now lives on the south coast. When he is not writing, he visits second-hand bookshops, watches videos of old Hollywood films, and takes long walks along empty beaches. He has also written *Kidnap!*, *The Big Story*, *A Pretty Face*, *Blackbeard*, and *The Wild West*, and has adapted *White Fang* for Dominoes.

OXFORD
UNIVERSITY PRESS

CONTENTS

BEFORE READING

1 **The stories in this book come from these countries. Match the countries and pictures.**

Britain

China

Hungary

Switzerland

the USA

2 **There are six stories in this book. Which of the five countries do they come from?**

   a Tom Blood takes the King's jewels from the Tower of London. ....

   b Lord Bao lives in a country in Asia. ....

   c Johnny Appleseed meets Abraham Lincoln. ....

   d William Tell lives in a country with lots of mountains. ....

   e Lady Godiva and Tom Blood come from the same country. ....

   f King Matthias lives in a country in the centre of Europe. ....

William Tell

William Tell lives near **Lake** Lucerne, in Switzerland, with his young son, Carl.

Every day, in the town near Tell's house, **Baron** Gessler makes everyone **bow** to his hat. They are all afraid of him.

lake a lot of water with land round it

baron an important man

bow to put down your head in front of someone or something important

One day, Tell and his son go to the town. They walk past the Baron's hat without bowing. Just then, Gessler arrives.

'What's this?' he says. 'Bow to my hat, you dogs!' 'Never!' says Tell. 'Take him!' shouts Gessler to his men.

'For this you must die, Tell!' cries Gessler angrily. But Tell is not afraid.

Then Gessler looks at the apple in his hand, and smiles. 'Wait . . . **Shoot** through this apple, my friend, and you can live.'

'All right,' says Tell.

shoot to hit something from far away

'Take the boy to that tree and put the apple on his head!' Baron Gessler tells his men, and he laughs. Tell takes two **arrows** out, and gets ready to shoot.

'You can do it, Father!' shouts Carl. 'Don't be afraid.'

William Tell shoots one arrow at his son, and . . .

. . . it goes through the apple and into the tree!

arrow you shoot things with this

'Why have you got a new arrow ready?' asks an angry Gessler.
'To shoot you, Baron,' says Tell.

'Take him to my **castle**!' Gessler tells his men angrily.

The Baron's men take Tell to a **boat** on the lake.
'Run, Carl!' shouts Tell to his son.

People throw things at the Baron. They aren't afraid of him any more.

When the boat is out on the lake, there's a bad **storm**.
'Let's get Tell to help us!' shout the Baron's men. 'He's good with boats.'

castle a big old building; a rich person lives here

boat you go across water in this

storm a lot of rain and very bad weather

So Tell **steers** the boat. But soon there are **rocks** in front of them!
'What are you doing?' Gessler shouts at him.

Tell **jumps** from the boat before it hits the rocks. Suddenly, Gessler and his men are in the water!

'You're a dead man, William Tell!' shouts the Baron angrily. 'And every man, woman and child in the town must die with you, too!'

Tell says nothing. He takes an arrow and shoots Gessler. The Baron **falls** into the lake – and does not come up again.

READING CHECK

Choose the correct pictures.

a . . . lives with his son
in Switzerland.

b Baron Gessler makes people
bow in front of his . . .

c The Baron makes Tell hit . . .

d The Baron wants to take Tell to . . .

e Tell takes the boat to . . .

f In the end Tell shoots . . .

WORD WORK

boat
bow   castle
fall   jump   storm
lake   steer
arrows   rocks   shoot

Write these sentences with words from the Baron's hat.

a You use this to ⬤ the car to the left or the right.

You use this to steer the car to the left or the right.

b Japanese people 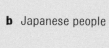 their heads when they meet.

....

c We swim or take a out on the when it's hot.

....

d He's a very rich man and he lives in a .

....

e There was a very bad last night.

....

f Don't off those !

....

g Take your and at that tree.

....

GUESS WHAT

The next story happens in England in the 1600s. What is it about? Tick the boxes.

The Tower
of London
YES ☐ NO ☐

A Tower Guard
YES ☐ NO ☐

King Charles II
YES ☐ NO ☐

Oxford
YES ☐ NO ☐

Tom Blood

Tom Blood arrives home after **fighting** in the English **Civil War**.

'Where are you?' he calls to his wife.

But there's nothing in the house, and his wife isn't there.

He looks at her picture. 'I must find her. But where? Perhaps she's in London!'

fighting when someone hits people again and again

civil war when half of a country fights with the other half

Tom goes to London to look for his wife, but no one can help him.

Then, after three long days, a man gives him some good **news**.

'She's living in that house over there,' he says.

Tom finds his wife in a small room. 'Why are you here?' he asks.

'We have no money, Tom,' she says. 'The **King** has our house, and all our things. His men are taking everything from the losers in the Civil War.'

news when someone tells you something new

king the most important man in a country

Tom is angry. 'The King **steals** everything from me,' he says. 'So I must steal something from him.'

The next day, Tom changes his **clothes**. 'Why are you wearing a **parson's** hat and coat?' his wife asks.

'We're going to the **Tower** of London,' he says with a smile.

They go to see the King's **jewels**. After that, Tom visits the Tower every day for a week.

Soon Talbot, the **guard**, is his friend, and Tom can visit the Tower after it closes. Talbot meets him at the door. 'Come in, parson,' he says.

In the jewel room one night, Tom hits Talbot on the head.

'Now for the jewels,' he thinks. And he puts them into his coat.

steal to take something without asking

clothes people wear these

parson a man who works in a church

tower a tall building

jewels a king wears these very expensive things on important days

guard a man who stops people from stealing things

Suddenly, lots of Tower guards come running in. 'The parson's stealing the jewels!' one of them **shouts**.

Later, the guards take Tom to the King. 'What do you have to say about this, Tom Blood?' he asks.

'You take all my things. Is that **fair**?' asks Tom.
'Yes!' says the King.
'Right! You take all my things, so I take your jewels,' says Tom. 'Is that fair?'

The king looks at Tom for a minute. Then he laughs. 'You're a **clever** man, Tom Blood!' he says. 'And I like you. You can have your things back. And from this day you can be one of the King's Men.'

shout to say loudly and angrily   **fair** good for all people   **clever** quick-thinking

ACTIVITIES

STORY CHECK

Put the sentences in order. Number them 1–9.

a ☐ The King takes everything in Blood's house.

b ☐ One night Blood takes the King's jewels from the Tower.

c ☐ At first Tom Blood fights in the Civil War.

d ☐ Blood finds Mrs Blood later in London.

e ☐ Blood makes friends with Talbot in the Tower of London.

f ☐ The King gives Blood's house and money back to him.

g ☐ Blood can't find his wife or his things when he comes home.

h ☐ Then the King's men find Blood in the Tower.

i ☐ They take him to the King and Blood and the king speak.

WORD WORK

1 Find thirteen more words from the story in the wordsquare.

G	H	U	F	A	D	I	X	J	O
F	L	O	C	L	O	T	H	E	S
I	K	B	U	S	C	Q	U	W	H
F	I	G	H	T	I	N	G	E	O
A	N	U	G	E	V	E	K	L	U
I	G	A	Z	A	I	W	I	S	T
R	O	R	B	L	L	S	Z	O	V
O	C	D	T	O	W	E	R	A	L
Y	L	V	U	P	A	R	S	O	N
C	L	E	V	E	R	F	H	I	J

ACTIVITIES

2 Use the words from Activity 1 to complete the sentences.

a Charles II was the ......King...... of England from 1660–85.

b A .... is when one half of a country is .... against the other half.

c An English .... usually wears black ....

d In a castle there is often a .... at the door to stop people.

e Something that you don't know is ....

f A .... person gives the same to everyone.

g A .... person can think quickly.

h Rich people like to wear expensive and beautiful ....

i The .... of London is a very old building.

j It's bad to .... things from shops.

k Don't ....! I can hear you.

GUESS WHAT

The next story comes from China. These are the people in the story. Are they good 😊 or bad 😞?

A judge

A poor boy

A servant

A man in black clothes

Lord Bao and the Stone

Lord Bao lives in the south of China. He is a **judge**, and all the people love him because he is very fair.

One day, he and his **servant** see a young boy in the town. The boy usually **sells oil** in the street, but now he is crying.

'Little boy, why are you crying?' asks Lord Bao.

lord an important man

Bao /baʊ/

judge a person who says when something is right or wrong

servant a person who works for someone rich

sell to take money for something

oil you cook things in this

'Every afternoon I put my head on this **stone** and have a sleep,' the boy says. 'I always put my money next to me. But now it isn't here!'

'I see,' says Lord Bao. 'So this stone is the **thief!**'

He shouts at the stone. 'Do you have this boy's money? Answer me!'

The people in the street listen and laugh. 'What is Lord Bao saying?' they cry. 'He's **mad!**'

stone something grey or white and hard

thief a person who takes things without asking

mad thinking things that are not true

Lord Bao turns to them. 'Are you calling me mad? I must **fine** every one of you a one cent **coin** for that!'

Eveyone stops laughing and Lord Bao's servant opens his bag. 'Put your coins in this,' says Lord Bao.

Without speaking, the people put their coins into the bag.

Lord Bao watches very carefully.

When a man in black puts his coin into the bag, Lord Bao looks up at him. 'You are the thief!' he says.

fine ask someone for money when they do something wrong

coin metal money

'But how do you know?' the people ask, with open mouths.

Lord Bao carefully takes the man's coin from the bag. 'Look at the oil on this!' he says. 'The boy is an oil seller and always has oil on his hands. So this is the boy's coin, and this man is the thief.'

The people turn angrily to the man in black, and he is afraid. He quickly takes all the boy's money from his coat and gives it back.

The little oil seller is very happy. 'Thank you, thank you,' he says to Lord Bao, and then he runs home.

The END

READING CHECK

Match the two parts of the sentences.

a   Lord Bao and his servant are . . .
b   A young boy there is . . .
c   The boy has no money because . . .
d   Lord Bao speaks . . .
e   All the people in the street . . .
f   Lord Bao asks them all . . .
g   Lord Bao sees the boy's money . . .
h   The man in black is . . .
i   The boy . . .

1   the thief.
2   angrily to a stone about this.
3   walking in the street.
4   because it has oil on it.
5   for money.
6   gets his money back.
7   crying.
8   laugh at him.
9   someone has his money.

WORD WORK

1   Find the words from the story.

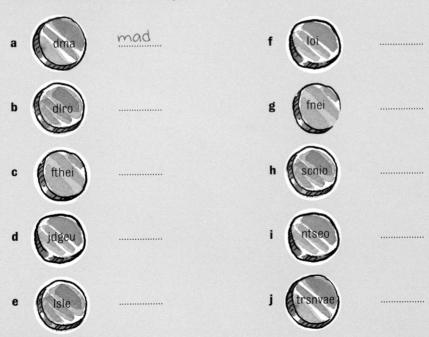

a   dma   mad

b   dlro   ....

c   fthei   ....

d   jdgeu   ....

e   lsle   ....

f   loi   ....

g   fnei   ....

h   scnio   ....

i   ntseo   ....

j   trsnvae ....

2 Use the words from Activity 1 to complete the sentences.

a That man works as the .... of a rich ....

b People think that the .... is .....mad..... because he speaks to a ....

c Lord Bao ....s all the people when they laugh.

d The .... gives all the .... back.

e 'Can I .... you some ....?' says the boy.

GUESS WHAT

The next story comes from Hungary. What happens? Tick the boxes.

a King Matthias is
   happy with . . .

one of his men. ☐   his wife. ☐   his castle. ☐

b The King
   of Prussia . . .

fights with Matthias. ☐   visits Matthias. ☐   shoots with Matthias. ☐

c The story ends
   well for . . .

the King of Prussia. ☐   King Matthias. ☐   the King of Prussia's
                                            daughter. ☐

The King of Prussia is visiting his friend **Matthias**, the King of Hungary. 'I hear you have a **sheep** with a **fleece** of **gold**,' he says. 'Is this true?'

King Matthias and the Good Shepherd

'Yes,' says Matthias. 'And I have a very good **shepherd**, too. He never **lies**.'
'I can make him lie,' says the King of Prussia with a smile.

'Do that, and half of Hungary is yours,' says Matthias. 'But I know my shepherd well, and no one can make him lie.'

'*I* can,' says the Prussian king. 'Or half of Prussia is *yours*, Matthias.'
'Very well,' says the Hungarian king.

Matthias /məˈθaɪəs/

sheep (*plural* **sheep**) an animal, usually white or black, that lives in the country

fleece the hairy coat of a sheep

gold an expensive yellow metal

shepherd a man who looks after sheep

lie to say something that is not true

20

The Prussian king changes his clothes. Then he goes to look for the shepherd.

The Prussian king says hello to the shepherd.
'Hello, king!' he answers.
'How do you know me in these clothes?'
'I can hear your **voice**,' says the shepherd.
'What do you want?'

'I have six horses for you,' says the Prussian king. 'But first you must give me the sheep with the fleece of gold.'
'No,' says the shepherd. 'I can't steal from King Matthias.'

'What about ten horses?' says the Prussian king.

'No,' answers the shepherd.
So the king goes back home to Prussia.

voice the noise that someone makes when they speak

...f Prussia goes home and
...aughter about the shepherd.
...e to talk to him,' she says.
...she takes a bag of gold and a
...ttle of **wine** with her.

'Look!' she says to the shepherd. 'I can give you a bag of gold for your sheep with the fleece of gold!'
'Never!' says the shepherd. 'I don't need your money.'

After some wine, he begins to feel very happy. 'All right,' he says. 'Take the sheep with the fleece of gold. But first you must give me a **kiss** and be my wife.'

'Very well. But I want only the sheep's fleece, not the **meat**.'

The girl takes the fleece back to her father. And the Prussian king is very happy.

wine a red or white drink; when you drink a lot you feel happy and sleepy

kiss to touch lovingly with your mouth

meat the part of an animal that people eat

The next morning, the shepherd goes to King Matthias. 'What can I tell him about the fleece?' he thinks. 'I don't want to lie.'

'Good morning!' says King Matthias to him. 'Where's the sheep with the fleece of gold?'

'I don't have it any more,' says the shepherd. 'Now I have a black sheep.'

'I see. And where is this black sheep?' asks Matthias angrily. 'Sitting next to you!' says the shepherd. And he looks at the Prussian king's daughter.

'Shepherd, you speak truly,' says Matthias. 'For that, you can have my half of Prussia.'

'And my daughter,' says the Prussian king. 'I can see you're in love with her.' And so, in time, the good shepherd **becomes** the next king of Prussia.

become to change from one thing to a different thing

ACTIVITIES

READING CHECK

Correct seven more mistakes in the story of King Matthias.

Prussia

The King of ~~France~~ is visiting King Matthias of Hungary. Matthias is happy because he has

a special black sheep and a very bad shepherd. Matthias says the Prussian king can have

half of Hungary for making the shepherd laugh. The Prussian king says he can do it or

Matthias can have all of Prussia. The Prussian king's daughter is nice to the shepherd. He

gives her the sheep's head, but he doesn't lie to King Matthias. In the end King Matthias

gives his quarter of Prussia to the shepherd and the Prussian king gives his daughter to

Matthias too.

WORD WORK

1 These words don't match the pictures. Correct them.

a   ~~sheep~~ ...gold........   d   gold ....

b   meat ....   e   wine ....

c   fleece ....   f   shepherd ....

2 Find the words in the shepherd's stick to match the underlined words.

beliea**gold**tvoicerikisscb e c o m e e

a I like <u>expensive yellow metal</u> watches. ....gold.....

b Don't <u>say something when it's not true</u>! ....

c I like her <u>noise when she speaks</u>. ....

d Let's <u>make our mouths meet</u>. ....

e Does he really <u>change into</u> the King of Prussia? ....

3 What are the extra letters in the shepherd's stick? Write them in order and find the name of King Matthias's wife. B _ _ _ _ _ _ _

GUESS WHAT

The next story comes from the United States. It starts in 1796.
What is it about? Tick three boxes.

Indians ☐

Oil in Texas ☐

Apple trees ☐

The first trains ☐

Abraham Lincoln ☐

It's September 1796, in a small country town in Pennsylvania, America.

A new baby, John Chapman, opens his eyes for the first time. He looks out of the window and sees an apple tree!

When John is a young man, he has a **dream**.

'I see a land full of apple trees!' he says. 'Nobody is hungry there, because there are apples for everyone!'

dream pictures that you see in your head

The next morning, John leaves home. His coat is an old **coffee sack**, and his hat is a **tin pot**. He takes with him only a **spade** and a bag of apple **seeds**.

John walks and walks. 'Over the hills, and across the **plain**. Under the sun and through the rain,' he sings.

And all the time, John **plants** apple seeds. 'Big trees come from little seeds,' he says.

At this time, many people in America are moving West. They are making new towns with shops and houses in them.

'You need trees too,' John tells the people in the new towns. And he plants his apple seeds there. The town people give him a new name – Johnny Appleseed!

coffee people often drink this in the morning

sack a big bag

tin a cheap white metal

pot you cook in this

spade you use this in the garden

seeds flowers and trees come from these

plain land with no hills

plant to put seeds in the land

Johnny is a good friend of the **Indians**, too.

One day, in a small town, John sees a young boy.

'Here, boy!' says John. 'Take these apple seeds and plant them.'
'Thank you,' says the boy.

'What's your name?' asks John.
'Abe,' says the boy. 'Abraham Lincoln.'

Indians they lived in North America before white people

28

Sometimes, years later, John goes back to a town or village. The people are always happy to see Johnny Appleseed again.

And when he sees his apple trees, he feels happy too.

When Johnny Appleseed is ill, the Indians help him to get well again.

The End

After many long years, John Chapman dies. But in towns and villages all across America, Johnny Appleseed's trees are alive today – and many have nice red apples on them now!

READING CHECK

Correct these sentences.

a John Chapman's story begins in ~~1896~~. *1796*

b When he's a boy he sees an apple tree out of his window.

c He wants to put flowers in every town in America.

d He leaves home in very usual clothes.

e He drives across America.

f He steals apples everywhere he goes.

g He meets George Washington when he's a boy.

h He dies after a long life of bad work.

WORD WORK

1 Find words from the story to match the pictures.

a c o f f e e   b d _ _ _ _ _   c p _ _ _ _ _

d p _ _   e l _ _ _ _ _ _ _   f s _ _ _ _   g s _ _ _ _ _ _

h s _ _ _ _ _   i t _ _   j p _ _ _ _ _

2 Use the words from Activity 1 to complete the sentences.

a People have ....dream..s every night, but they often forget them.

b There are no hills near here, just a big ....

c I usually drink .... at breakfast time.

d What's in the .... on your back? Jewels or gold?

e Where's the ....? I want to do some work in the garden.

f That coin isn't gold; it's ....!

g Is there any hot water in the ....?

h Pocahontas is an .... name.

i When you .... these .... in your garden, you get red flowers.

GUESS WHAT

**The next story happens in Britain.
Here are two of the people in it.
Tick the boxes.**

Who . . .

Lady Godiva

Earl Leofric

a . . . is rich?		
b . . . lives in a castle?		
c . . . wants to help people.		
d . . . wants to get more money.		
e . . . gets angry.		
f . . . wears no clothes in the street one day.		
g . . . loses money in the end.		

This is the town of Coventry in England in 1057. Many people there are **poor** because of all the **taxes**.

Earl Leofric doesn't listen to the cries of the poor people.

At the Earl's castle, his wife, **Lady Godiva**, is angry. 'You must stop all these taxes!' she tells him.

poor without money

taxes money that people give to the important men in their country

earl an important man

Leofric /ˈliːəʊfrɪk/

lady the wife of an earl

Godiva /gəˈdaɪvə/

'To stop the taxes you must **ride naked** through the streets of Coventry!' he says. And he laughs.

But his wife is not laughing. 'Very well,' she says. 'But are you happy for me to do this?'
'Y . . . yes,' says Leofric.

Lady Godiva meets the town **councillors** and tells them the news. 'Dear Lady, you can't do it!' they say.
'Oh, yes, I can,' she says. Then she goes back to Leofric.

'When she rides through the city, people must stay in their houses,' the councillors say. 'They must close their doors and windows. Nobody must see her.'

Soon everyone is talking about Lady Godiva.
'She wants to ride naked through the town!' they say.
'Is it true?'

ride to go on a horse

naked without clothes

councillors the important men that look after a town

The day comes when Godiva must ride through Coventry. Her servants take her clothes. 'My Lady!' they say. 'How can you do this?' '*I must* do it for the poor people of Coventry,' she tells them.

So Lady Godiva rides through the streets. Everyone is at home. No windows or doors are open. There is nobody to see her.

One man is working in his shop. His name is Tom, and he makes clothes.

Out in the street, Lady Godiva goes past on her horse. Suddenly, the horse **neighs**. Tom hears it in his shop.

neigh the noise that a horse makes

He opens his window and looks out. And Lady Godiva sees him looking at her.

Suddenly Tom becomes **blind**. 'Help! I can't see!' he cries.

Soon Lady Godiva arrives back at the castle. She puts on her clothes, then goes to her husband.

'Now can you stop those taxes, my Lord?' she says.
'Yes, my Lady,' says Earl Leofric. 'But the taxes on horses must stay!' (He knows about the horse's neigh, you see!)

blind when a person cannot see

READING CHECK

Choose the correct words to complete the sentences.

a Many people in Coventry have got/haven't got a lot of money.

b Leofric is/isn't interested in the poor people's problems.

c Leofric's wife Godiva is angry/happy with him.

d To help the poor, Leofric says Godiva must go through Coventry
with no/expensive clothes on.

e Her friends in the town say nobody must look/laugh at her.

f One man looks out of his door/window when she goes past.

g In the end Godiva helps Leofric/the people of Coventry.

WORD WORK

Use the words in Lady Godiva's hair to complete the sentences on page 37.

lady ride neigh earl blind naked taxes councillor poor

PROJECT A

A folk hero

1 Read about this folk heroine. Complete the table.

JOAN OF ARC

Joan of Arc is a folk heroine in France. In French stories Joan is brave and she fights against the English. In this picture she is wearing armour and she has short hair. Her friends are Gilles de Rais and The King of France. The English are her enemies.

Joan of Arc

Name	Joan of Arc
Country	
Character	
Actions	
Appearance	
Friends	
Enemies	